Festivals

of the Christian year

Lois Rock

LION
Children's Books

To Luke and Bethany

This edition copyright © 1996 Lion Publishing
Illustrations copyright © 1996 Susan Hutchison

Photography by John Williams Studios, Thame
Text and artefacts by Lois Rock
Painting on spreads 3 and 20 by Nicky Jex

The author asserts the moral right to be identified
as the author of this work

Published by
Lion Publishing plc
Sandy Lane West, Oxford, England
www.lion-publishing.co.uk
ISBN 0 7459 3456 0

The quote of Saint Francis on spread 20 is taken
from 'Francis' Letter to the Faithful', quoted in *St
Francis of Assisi: An Omnibus of Sources*, edited by
Marion A. Habig (SPCK, 2nd edition 1979); the story
of Francis and the birds is adapted from 'The First
Life of St Francis by Thomas of Celano', in the same
omnibus.

First edition 1996
10 9 8 7 6 5 4 3 2

A catalogue record for this book is available from
the British Library

Printed and bound in Malaysia

Christian Festivals

Festivals are special celebrations and Christians have lots of different ones in a year. Each festival helps them remember something important about their faith. For example:

- **God**. Christians believe God made the world and everything in it. They take time to thank God for this.

- **Jesus Christ**. Jesus is the one whom Christians follow. They believe he was God come as a human to mend the friendship between God and people—a friendship which had been broken since the beginning of time.

- **Being a Christian**. Jesus showed people how to live as friends of God. That makes a difference to what they do. Some of the special days in the Christian year remind people of this, and the season that follows gives them time to think, to learn and to let their lives be changed.

- **Learning from other Christians**. Some Christians are shining examples of how to follow Jesus. Special days are set aside for others to think about them and learn from the story of their life. These Christians are sometimes called saints.

CONTENTS

1 Advent

The Christian year starts with a season called Advent. The word means 'coming'. It is the time for looking forward to the coming of Christmas. At that time, Christians remember the birth of a baby named Jesus—a Jewish boy, born in the region that today is shared between Israel and Palestine. Christians believe that Jesus was God come to earth to make all people God's people.

Advent begins four Sundays before Christmas.

An Advent ring

Christians sometimes make an Advent ring for their church or their home. They light the candles to help count the weeks to Christmas.

On the first Sunday, they light one candle and let it burn for a few minutes—perhaps while they sing an Advent carol. Or they might listen to a reading from the book of the faith, the Bible, telling about some of the Jewish people who looked forward to the time when God would send someone to help them live as God's people.

On the second Sunday in Advent, Christians do the same, but light two candles; on the third Sunday, three; and on the last Sunday in Advent, they light four.

On Christmas Day, they light all the candles: the centre one reminds them that Jesus has come, bringing good news that lights up their lives.

An Advent song for little children

See the candle burning bright,
One by one each week we light.
Advent is the time to wait,
Then it's time to celebrate.
When the waiting time is through,
Christmas joy for me and you.

Tune: Twinkle, Twinkle, Little Star

Make it!

You will need

- *deep dish*
- *damp sand*
- *four coloured candles*
- *one taller white candle*
- *evergreens*

What to do

1 Fill the dish with damp sand.

2 Push the white candle into the centre.

3 Push the coloured candles into the sand around the edge.

4 Push the evergreens in all around to hide the side. Keep them clear of the wick.

5 Keep the sand moist by watering it a little each day through Advent.

2 Saint Nicholas

'Love God and one another.'

That is what Jesus told people in what he said and what he did. His followers want to obey.

Hundreds of years ago, a Christian named Nicholas showed his love and care for one poor family by giving them gifts of money. He didn't want thanks or a big fuss, so he gave the money secretly, by throwing it through a window!

Some Christians celebrate the feast of Saint Nicholas on his special day—6 December—by giving secret gifts then. Others celebrate the giving of secret gifts on Christmas night.

Gifts given secretly

Saint Nicholas, is best known by the Dutch way of saying his name: Santa Claus.

Some people hang up a stocking like this, hoping that Santa Claus—or some secret gift bringer—will fill it with good things!

Make it!

You will need

- *coloured felt*
- *coloured yarn*
- *needle*
- *scissors*

What to do

1 Cut a piece of felt in a stocking shape. Cut another exactly the same.

2 Cut two rectangles, each about 6 cm deep, as a border for the top of each side of the stocking.

3 Thread the needle and knot the end. Push the needle through the double border from the wrong side. Make a fancy pattern of stitches. Do this to both pieces.

4 Put the pieces together, right side out. Ask a grown-up to make a strong starting stitch, and then take small stitches all round the edge. Ask a grown-up to make a strong finishing stitch.

5 Make a loop of thread in the top corner to hang the stocking.

What gifts would you like to find in a stocking? What gifts can you make or buy to give a friend?

3 The Christmas Baby

Christmas is the time when Christians celebrate the birth of the baby Jesus.

Christians remember the story in many ways: in plays, in pictures, and in models.

A crib scene

This model helps tell the Christmas story. It shows—

Mary, the village girl who was told by an angel that she would have a special baby, God's son.

Joseph, who married Mary and promised to look after her and the baby.

The stable, the room where Mary's baby was born.

The manger, the feed box for animals that Mary used as a cradle.

The baby Jesus.

An angel, like the ones who appeared to shepherds out on the hillside nearby, saying that God's special baby was born.

The shepherds, the ordinary working people who were the first to hear the news and who came to the stable to see.

Make it!

You will need

- *thin card*
- *coloured markers*
- *scissors*
- *glue*
- *sticky putty*

What to do

1 Draw a shape like this on thin card.

2 Draw the manger scene, showing Mary and Joseph, the animals in the stable and the baby in the manger.

3 Cut out the shape. Fold the sides as marked and glue the tabs to the back of them.

4 Draw shepherds on more card.

5 Cut out each shape with a tab as shown here. Slit the tab and fold one half forward and the other half back so that the figure stands up.

6 Draw an angel. Cut it out and use sticky putty to attach it to the scene.

4 The Christmas Tree

Jesus, the Christmas baby, grew up. Then he began a very special task: showing people just how much God loved them. His followers found out that what he said was true. They discovered God was truly with them as a special friend. They believed they would be safe with God for ever—even after death.

They began to show how much they loved God by loving others all around them.

Hundreds of years later, a Christian named Boniface did something kind that made the fir tree a Christian symbol from that day to this.

The legend of Saint Boniface and the fir tree

Long ago, a Christian named Boniface set out on a special mission. He wanted people all through Europe to hear about Jesus and the good news about how much God loved them.

In those days, people worshipped other gods. One day, Boniface came across a group of people who had tied a young boy to an oak tree as part of their worship. They were going to kill him to try to please their cruel god.

Boniface stopped them. He told them of his God—a God of gentleness and love.

Then he cut down the oak tree. There, by its stump, was a tiny fir tree.

'Look at this tree,' said Boniface. 'Its leaves are always green: let them remind you that God loves you for ever.

'Look at how it points to the sky. Let it remind you to trust in God above.'

Make it!

You will need

- craft foil
- scissors
- pencil
- card
- sticky tape
- cotton thread

What to do

1 Copy the shapes shown here onto card.

2 Draw round the card to mark the outline on the craft foil. Cut out.

3 Make the lanterns by folding the rectangle of foil in half and making a row of snips along the folded edge.

4 Open up the foil and curl round your finger to make the lantern. Tape in place on the inside.

5 Use tiny pieces of tape to stick a handle to the top.

6 To make the stars, follow the step-by-step instructions.

7 Finally, cut short pieces of thread, fold them into loops, and tape them to the stars to hang them.

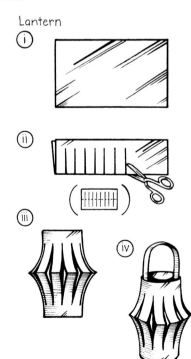

Lantern

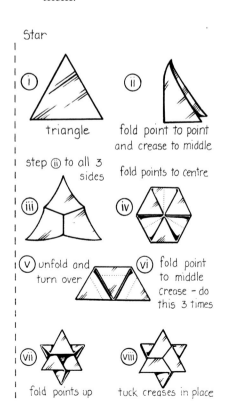

Star

(i) triangle

(ii) fold point to point and crease to middle

(iii) step (ii) to all 3 sides

(iv) fold points to centre

(v) unfold and turn over

(vi) fold point to middle crease – do this 3 times

(vii) fold points up

(viii) tuck creases in place

A tree and its decorations

Today, Christians use fir trees (and other evergreens) as part of their Christmas decorations. Sometimes, the decorations they put on have a special meaning too. Here are two decorations often hung on Christmas trees:

Stars—*like the one that led wise men to the baby Jesus.*

Lanterns—*real ones light the dark night, just as the good news of God's love lights up a dark and sad world.*

5 Epiphany

Twelve days after Christmas comes a festival called Epiphany. The word comes from a Greek word meaning 'showing'. Christians celebrate the time when the baby Jesus was shown to people from other countries.

These were wise men, who came to Bethlehem from other lands far to the East. They brought rich gifts to show how important they believed him to be.

It was the first hint that Jesus had not come just for the Jewish people—but for all people everywhere.

A display of three gifts is a good way to mark Epiphany.

Make it!

You will need

- **gift-sized boxes and containers**
- **masking tape**
- **gesso**
- **acrylic paints in rich colours: gold, silver, red, blue, purple, jade**
- **brushes**
- **scissors**

What to do

1 Choose three differently-shaped containers for your three gifts. Use masking tape to tape extra bits on, if you wish.
2 Brush gesso all over the gift (except the base) and leave to dry.
3 Paint in rich colours of your choosing.

If you have made the crib scene on page 3, Epiphany is the time to make 'wise men' bringing gifts. Draw them in richly-coloured clothes and add them to the scene.

Three gifts

The gifts the wise men brought Jesus each had a special meaning.

One was **gold**, a gift for a king. When he grew up, people came to believe that Jesus was a king sent by God.

One was **frankincense**, the hardened sap of a plant. Frankincense burns with a sweet-smelling scent. It was used by priests in ceremonies to worship God. The gift showed that Jesus was going to be a priest— someone who makes a bridge between people and God.

The other was **myrrh**. This was another type of resin, from a different sort of plant. It has a strong smell. People who could afford to sprinkled it among the bandages used to wrap round a dead body being got ready for burial. It was a hint that Jesus' death was going to be a special one.

The Light of the world

Epiphany is also a time to celebrate the belief that Jesus' message of love is for all the world. The Christingle reminds people of this in several ways:

The orange stands for the world.

The fruits are a reminder of the good things the world provides.

The red band is a reminder that Jesus died and his blood was shed to show God's love to the world.

The candle is a reminder that Jesus, with his message of love and forgiveness, is light for the whole world.

To make a Christingle, simply cut a hole in an orange with an apple corer. Wrap kitchen foil around the base of the candle and push it into the hole. Fan the foil out prettily. Next, wrap red ribbon (or a strip of red paper) around the orange and sticky-tape it into place. Last, thread fruits onto four cocktail sticks and stick these into the orange.

6 Shrove Tuesday

Halfway through the winter—about six weeks before Easter—comes the season of Lent. The 40 days of Lent remember a special time in Jesus' life. He grew up and worked as a builder-carpenter. Then, he began a new work—telling people about God. To get ready, he spent 40 days alone in the desert, going without food and thinking of all that lay ahead.

It is a time when Christians try to live more simply than usual so they have time to think about God, too. But first comes a feast, to use up any rich foods! This is Shrove Tuesday.

Games with pancakes

TOSS THE PANCAKE

1 Give all the players a frying pan and a cooked pancake.
2 Toss the pancake.
3 The aim is to shake the pan to toss the pancake up and over. Who can toss the pancakes the most times in a minute?

PANCAKE RACE

Who can run a course fastest while tossing a pancake a set number of times as they run?

A rich feast

In days gone by, the rich foods people had were creamy milk and eggs. They used these to make pancakes before the start of Lent.

Why not have a pancake feast? Try serving warm pancakes with your choice of yummy toppings.

a spoonful of cream and a trickle of chocolate sauce

a sprinkle of sugar and a squeeze of lemon juice

You will need

- **150 g self-raising flour**
- **25 g butter**
- **25 g caster sugar**
- **2 eggs**
- **about 400 ml milk**
- **extra butter**
- **bowl**
- **whisk**
- **frying pan**
- **spatula**

What to do

1 Put the flour in a bowl. Add the butter and 'rub it in'—break it up into tiny pieces with your fingers.

2 Add the sugar. Mix.

3 Make a hollow in the centre of the flour and break the eggs into it. Stir gently in the hollow. Slowly work the spoon round to the edges of the hollow and mix in the flour bit by bit.

4 Add the milk splash by splash as you mix, so the mixture is always sticky and soft. Then stir in enough of the rest of the milk to give you a batter as thick as double cream.

5 Melt a little butter in a frying pan over a medium heat. Add a spoonful of the mixture, which will flatten out to make a small pancake.

6 Watch the bubbles form on the top and them burst. Now slip the spatula underneath and flip the pancake over. Let it cook for a minute or so to brown the other side.

7 Make more pancakes in the same way.

sliced peaches and strawberry jam

maple syrup

7 Ash Wednesday and Lent

After the feasting and fun of Shrove Tuesday comes a season for quiet thinking. There are about six weeks to go to the great festival of Easter. Christians want to spend the time thinking about Jesus: what does it mean to follow him? What kind of difference does it make? They long to discover more about God and God's love, and to let their lives be changed by it so they can show more of God's love to others.

Burning up the bad

When something is burned up, only ashes are left. On Ash Wednesday, Christians use ashes as a symbol of being sorry for wrongdoing and wanting to get rid of it for ever. In days gone by, people wore sackcloth and ashes on this day as a sign of being sorry. Nowadays, in some churches, there are special services when the leader smudges a little ash on people's foreheads.

The sign of the cross

These Lenten bookmarks have been decorated with a cross. It is the most important symbol of the Christian faith. You can find out why by reading pages 11 and 12.

Make it!

You will need

- **hessian**
- **scissors**
- **needle**
- **coloured yarn**
- **pencil**
- **squared paper**

What to do

1 Cut a bookmark shape from hessian.
2 On squared paper, work out a design using some of the stitches shown here, or ones you make up yourself.

3. Thread the needle and work the design on hessian. Leave a long tail of thread when you start to sew, and end with a long tail. Ask a grown-up to help you weave these tails into the back of the stitches on the wrong side of the bookmark.

The book of the faith

During Lent, Christians spend extra time learning about their faith. Many Christians read the Bible every day of the year, but in Lent they may read more than usual, or they may take time to read other books about the faith.

Often, Christians will meet together to talk about their faith and to pray to God.

8 Mothering Sunday

The fourth Sunday in Lent is a time for a little celebration in the middle of a season of plain living.

For hundreds of years, there has been a tradition of going to the 'Mother Church' of the area on this day—perhaps the nearest really big church, or even the cathedral of the area. People would give thanks for the church—the group of Christians meeting to learn and to worship together—which helps them grow in their faith. It became a day for giving thanks to mothers, too.

Posy

In many churches, posies are made for children to give their mothers.

Make it!

FRUIT SALAD

You will need

- **apple and pear**
- **lemon**
- **15 ml caster sugar**
- **lemon squeezer**
- **fruit knife**
- **a little near-boiling water**
- **cup**
- **bowl**

What to do

1 Put the sugar in a cup. Add a little near-boiling water and stir to dissolve the sugar.
2 Squeeze half the lemon and add the juice. (Keep the other half for the biscuits.)
3 Cut the apple and pear into quarters and cut out the cores.
4 Chop the rest into chunks and put into a bowl. Pour over the juice mixture and stir to cover all the pieces of fruit in a little of the juice.

Make it!

MARZIPAN BISCUITS

You will need

- *150 g ground almonds*
- *150 g caster sugar*
- *juice of half a lemon*
- *1 egg white*
- *a baking tray lined with parchment*
- *a deep plate filled with icing sugar*

What to do

1 Preheat the oven to 160°C.
2 Put the dry ingredients into a bowl.
3 Add the egg white and lemon juice. Mix to form a paste.
4 Shape into small balls. Roll these in icing sugar.
5 Place on the baking tray and bake for 8-9 minutes.
6 Ask a grown-up to help you lift them from the oven. Wear oven mitts.

A treat to eat
Here is a special surprise to make for those mothers who usually get the meals ready.

9 Palm Sunday

Palm Sunday is the day when Christians remember a big parade, close to the end of Jesus' life.

Three years had passed since the time Jesus went into the desert to think about his new work of telling people about God. In that time he made many friends.

Some people loved him, because they had been sick, and he had healed them with a touch.

Others had been lonely: the bad things they did left them with no friends; but Jesus welcomed them, forgave them the bad things they had done and told them they could make a new start as God's friends.

Still others just enjoyed listening to the stories he told. They were good stories, the sort you can't forget—and they made you think about people and about God.

Some people had other hopes. Jesus was popular. He cared more about God than what people said about him. Perhaps he was going to set his people free from the Romans who ruled the land, who had no respect for God. Perhaps.

At this time, Jesus was travelling to the capital city, Jerusalem. He and his followers were going to celebrate a religious festival by the temple there. Thousands of other people were coming from all over the country—and from all over the Roman Empire.

As Jesus rode in on a donkey, people welcomed him with a great parade, waving branches from the trees nearby, and throwing their cloaks on the ground as a carpet.

'Hosanna, hosanna!' they shouted. The word means 'save us, we pray.'

A great parade

Today many Christians have a Palm Sunday procession—often with someone dressed as Jesus riding on a donkey. Some churches buy palm branches, but most people cut branches from trees that grow well in the area where they live. Or you can make paper palm leaves to wave.

Make it!

You will need

- **green paper**
- **green flower sticks**
- **scissors**
- **sticky tape**

What to do

1 Cut palm leaf shapes from green paper.
2 Tape a flower stick to the centre of each leaf shape.

A CARPET OF CLOAKS

People in Jesus' day usually wore simple tunics with a belt.

They also had rectangular cloaks, worn like this:

10 Maundy Thursday

Jesus' arrival in Jerusalem for a Jewish religious festival is remembered on Palm Sunday. A few days later, on Maundy Thursday, Christians remember how Jesus shared one of the festival meals with his closest followers.

The room was ready and everyone had arrived—but who was going to be the servant and wash everyone's dusty feet?

While Jesus' friends were arguing, Jesus himself took the bowl and towel and washed their feet. He told his followers that they must be ready to show their love for one another in humble ways like this.

'I'm giving you a new commandment,' he said. 'Love one another, as I have loved you.'

The Latin word for commandment, 'mandatum', is where the word Maundy comes from.

Make it!

You will need

- *piece of old vinyl flooring or a doormat wrapped in a bin liner*
- *a large plate or an old tray*
- *poster paint and brush*
- *paper to print on*
- *bowl of water, soap and an old towel*

What to do

1 Get the flooring or mat out first. As this activity can be messy, work in a room with an easy-to-wash floor. Lay out the paper to print on close by.

2 Put a generous amount of paint on the plate or tray and brush it out to form a fairly thick layer, large enough for you to put your foot in quite flat.

3 Place your bare foot in the paint, then step onto the piece of paper to make a footprint.

4 Step onto the flooring.

5 Now make a print with the other foot.

6 Wash your feet!

Serving one another

Because Jesus washed his disciples' feet, some Christians actually wash one another's feet in church services on Maundy Thursday. It is a reminder that they must serve one another in everyday ways all through the year, even if it means doing humble jobs.

After you have done this activity, you will have a good reason to find out how it actually feels to wash one another's feet!

Following Jesus

These footprints are a reminder to Christians of Jesus' invitation, 'Follow me!' Christians believe they should follow in Jesus' footsteps, living and loving as he did.

The Last Supper

At the meal, Jesus took bread and broke it for his friends to share.

'This is my body,' he said, 'broken for you.'

Then he took the cup of wine and passed it round.

'This is my blood,' he said, 'shed for you.'

He was telling them that he was going to die, but that they must share bread and wine to remember him.

Christians celebrate this sharing of bread and wine all through the Christian year. But on Maundy Thursday it seems even more special.

11 Good Friday

Jesus had many friends. There were also people who hated him.

A number of the religious leaders did. They were angry at what he said about God. They believed they were the experts in telling people how to live as God wanted. Yet Jesus told people the wrong they did was forgiven. How dare he?

They had a plan. Many of Jesus' own people, the Jews, wanted him to lead an army of his followers against the Romans. Jewish rebels had done so before. If they could get the Roman governor to believe Jesus was that sort of rebel, he would be sentenced to death.

On Thursday night, after the meal, one of Jesus' close friends, Judas, told the religious leaders where to find Jesus. They came and took him. They told lies about him to the Roman governor, Pontius Pilate.

He was condemned to be nailed to a cross of wood and left to die: crucified.

The Roman soldiers who were ordered to execute him made fun of him first. He was accused of wanting to be a rebel leader—'King of the Jews'. So they dressed him in a purple robe (the colour worn by kings) and made a crown of thorns for his head.

Jesus didn't fight back. Later, as he hung dying on the cross, he asked God to forgive those who were killing him.

You will need

- **3-5 bendy thorn branches about 90 cm long**
- **raffia or string**
- **a bucket half full of warm water**
- **gardening gloves**

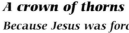

A crown of thorns

Because Jesus was forced to wear a crown of thorns, on Good Friday, Christians sometimes make a crown of thorns to remember how much he suffered. They take more trouble than the soldiers did!

What to do

1 Ask a grown-up to help you make this crown of thorns.
2 Wearing gloves, tie the branches together so they overlap.
3 Lower them into the warm water. As the water softens the branches, bend them in to make a circle, and push it to the bottom of the bucket.

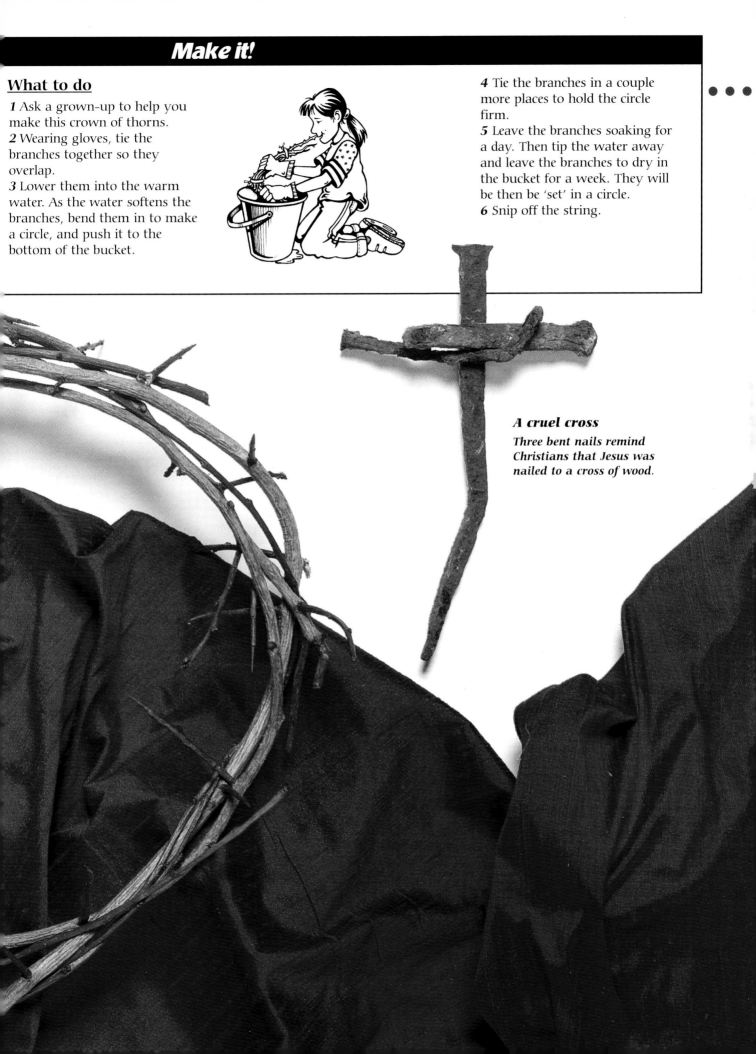

4 Tie the branches in a couple more places to hold the circle firm.
5 Leave the branches soaking for a day. Then tip the water away and leave the branches to dry in the bucket for a week. They will be then be 'set' in a circle.
6 Snip off the string.

A cruel cross

Three bent nails remind Christians that Jesus was nailed to a cross of wood.

12 Easter: The tomb in the garden

Jesus died on the cross. Two brave men went to ask for the body: a wealthy man named Joseph of Arimathea and a religious leader who admired Jesus, Nicodemus.

They had the body taken to a tomb Joseph owned: a cave cut in the rock, in a garden.

Jesus' friends had to hurry: the Jewish day of rest was beginning. They had to wrap the body quickly in strips of cloth, as was the custom; place the body on a ledge in the tomb; and roll the heavy stone in place as a door.

Three days later, women who were friends of Jesus came back to do the burial properly. But the stone door was open. The cloth was in place, but the body was gone.

Two shining figures appeared. 'A tomb is for dead bodies,' they said. 'Why look here for someone who is alive. Jesus isn't here. He has risen.'

Later, Jesus' friends saw him alive.

Christians celebrate the news: God's love is stronger than death. They believe that all Jesus had said about God's forgiveness and God's love must be true.

An Easter garden

This miniature garden with a tomb is something you will see in many churches to remember Jesus' coming back to life. And that is what Christians celebrate at Easter.

This garden needs 4–5 weeks to grow. You can start it early in Lent.

You will need

- **a deep tray**
- **an old stocking**
- **potting compost**
- **grass seed**
- **small spring-flowering plants, such as miniature daffodils, pansies or primroses, and trailing ivy**
- **a small flowerpot**
- **a large round stone that covers the opening of the flowerpot**
- **gravel**
- **twigs and raffia**

What to do

1 Mix the soil with lots of grass seed.

2 Put some soil in the tray and lay the flowerpot on its side in the centre.

3 Put some more of the seed and soil mix in the stocking. Shape it into a 'hill' on the tray, with the flowerpot at the base to be a 'tomb'.

4 Plant the plants in the soil in the tray. Water well. Water every few days to keep the soil moist.

5 After about 3 weeks the grass will start to grow. You can trim it carefully with scissors if needed, so it doesn't get too long.

6 For an Easter display, put the round stone just rolled away from the door, and a gravel path leading to it.

7 Use the twigs and raffia to make three crosses and push these into the top of the hill.

★ You may choose not to add the flowering plants until the day you want to display the garden, so you can be sure you have ones that are at their prettiest. In this case, grow them in pots and then transplant them into the garden, taking care not to spoil the grass as you wedge them in. Or you can simply push small bottles into the soil, fill them with water and add cut flowers.

13 Easter: New life

Christians believe that Jesus rose to new life at Easter.

They believe the promise he gave his followers: those who believe in Jesus and live as friends of God are forgiven all the wrong they have done. They will live as friends of God for ever.

Even though their bodies will die, they will enjoy new life with God.

Easter is in springtime, and the signs of new life in nature remind them of the new life God offers.

An Easter tree

In spring, chicks hatch from eggs that look as dead as stones. Some people decorate real eggs for Easter. Some give chocolate eggs with a surprise inside. Here, decorated half-shells have been filled with tiny gifts and hung on branches to make an Easter tree.

Make it!

You will need

- *empty egg shells*
- *gesso*
- *straws and a mug*
- *acrylic paints*
- *paintbrush*
- *stencil brush*
- *a piece of stiff card*
- *gift ribbon*
- *sticky tape*
- *tissue paper*
- *tiny Easter gifts*
- *a flowerpot filled with sand and stuck with bare branches*
- *bottle with cork*

1 Paint the outside of the egg shells with gesso and hang on the straws to dry.

2 Paint them with acrylic. Leave to dry.

3 Place a painted shell on an old bottle with a cork in the top. Dip the stencil brush in a different colour of paint; hold it bristle-end up near the egg shell and pull the stiff card across the bristles to make the paint fly off.

4 Turn the bottle round every couple of flicks so you spatter paint all round the egg.

5 When the paint is dry, cut lengths of gift ribbon and tape the ends gently inside the egg, to make a handle. Gently tuck a small piece of tissue paper in the egg. Add a gift.

6 Hang the eggs on the branches.

14 Pentecost

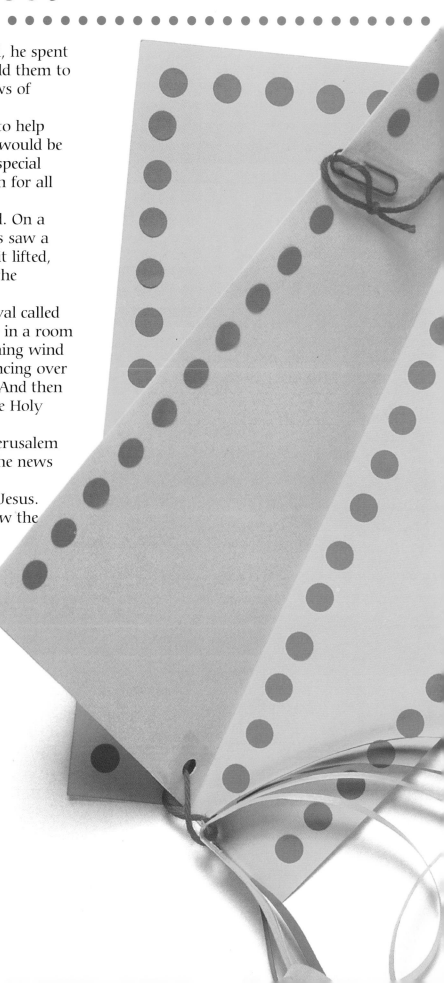

After Jesus rose from the dead, he spent forty days with his followers. He told them to take good news to all the world: news of God's love.

Jesus said that he would be there to help them, in a new and special way. He would be with them as the Holy Spirit, like a special friend inside giving help and strength for all they did.

But first, he had to go back to God. On a hilltop near Jerusalem, Jesus' friends saw a cloud wrap itself round him. When it lifted, Jesus had gone. This event is called the Ascension.

Ten days later came a Jewish festival called Pentecost. Jesus' closest friends were in a room together. Then something like a rushing wind blew. It seemed that flames were dancing over their heads—but they did not burn. And then they knew God's strength inside. The Holy Spirit had come.

They went out into the street in Jerusalem and for the first time began telling the news about Jesus.

Many people became followers of Jesus. From that day on, all Christians knew the Holy Spirit as a helper too.

Wind and flame

Flying a kite reminds Christians of the wind that blew at the first Pentecost. Rather like the Holy Spirit, wind is unseen, but very strong.

Red, yellow and orange streamers flutter like the flames that danced on the first Pentecost, and set Jesus' followers on fire with zeal to tell of their faith.

The dancing kite reminds them of the joy of having the Holy Spirit to help each one of them.

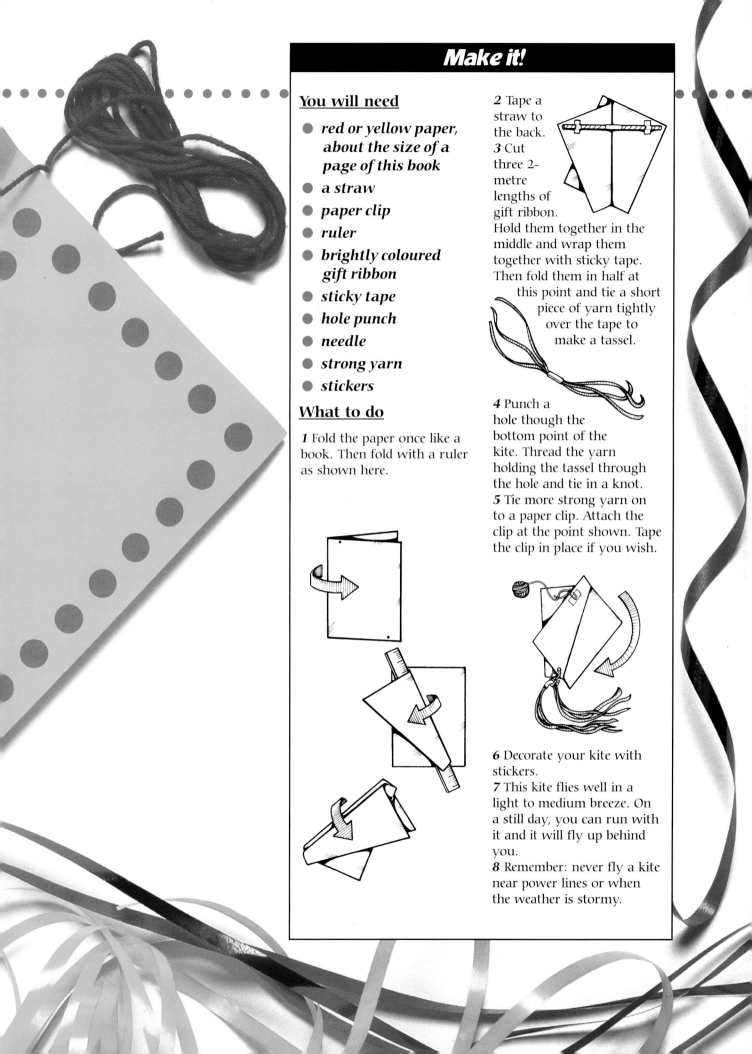

Make it!

You will need

- *red or yellow paper, about the size of a page of this book*
- *a straw*
- *paper clip*
- *ruler*
- *brightly coloured gift ribbon*
- *sticky tape*
- *hole punch*
- *needle*
- *strong yarn*
- *stickers*

What to do

1 Fold the paper once like a book. Then fold with a ruler as shown here.

2 Tape a straw to the back.

3 Cut three 2-metre lengths of gift ribbon. Hold them together in the middle and wrap them together with sticky tape. Then fold them in half at this point and tie a short piece of yarn tightly over the tape to make a tassel.

4 Punch a hole though the bottom point of the kite. Thread the yarn holding the tassel through the hole and tie in a knot.

5 Tie more strong yarn on to a paper clip. Attach the clip at the point shown. Tape the clip in place if you wish.

6 Decorate your kite with stickers.

7 This kite flies well in a light to medium breeze. On a still day, you can run with it and it will fly up behind you.

8 Remember: never fly a kite near power lines or when the weather is stormy.

15 Trinity

After Pentecost, Christians began to see that the one God they worshipped was known to them in three different ways:

● **God 'the Father'**—the God who made the world and everything in it. When Jesus told his followers how to pray, he told them to call God 'Father' or 'Daddy'.

● **God 'the Son'**—Jesus himself, God born as a human, who came to show people what it means to live as God's children.

● **God 'the Holy Spirit'**—God with them and in them as an unseen friend, helping them live as God's people ought.

A special way is used to describe the God who is three-in-one: Trinity.

Not long after Pentecost, some churches name a Sunday 'Trinity Sunday'.

The growing season

After Trinity Sunday comes a long season called Trinity. It is a time for Christians to grow in their understanding of God.

Three in one

These Christian symbols of the Trinity have three main shapes—a reminder of God as Father, Son and Holy Spirit. The one circle without beginning or end is a symbol of one God whose love goes on for ever. You will see symbols like these in many church buildings.

A clover leaf can be used as a Trinity symbol.

Make it!

You will need

● **modelling clay**

● **rolling pin**

● **blunt knife or modelling tool**

● **paints and brushes**

What to do

1 Roll out a lump of clay. Cut a circle or triangle to use as the base of your symbol.
2 Take a smaller piece of clay and roll out a long thin 'snake'.

Join the ends to make a big circle—big enough to fit easily all round the base. Rub over the join to make it smooth.
3 Now lay it on the base and loop it in one of the designs shown so the one circle makes three shapes, all the same size. Press the design down so it sticks well to the base.
4 Leave the clay to harden (or bake it if necessary). When it is dry, paint it.

16 Harvest

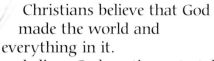

Christians believe that God made the world and everything in it.

They believe God continues to take care of the world. That is why there is sun and rain, summer and winter, seed-time and harvest.

In this way, God provides food and many other things people and animals need to live.

So they thank God for it.

In days gone by, people brought to church some of the things they had grown on their own farms and gardens. It was made into a wonderful display to remind them of the harvest God had given them.

Nowadays, only a few people grow their own food. More people earn money and buy food. So they bring foods they have bought, and also give money.

They still thank God for providing all they need.

And they share what they have, sending gifts of food and money to others.

Harvest gifts

A harvest gift box, full of good things from the garden and kitchen. Christians thank God for all the harvests in the world, and share the good things they have with those in need.

You will need

- *a large piece of corrugated cardboard*
- *ruler and pencil*
- *wool, string or raffia (or all three)*
- *safety craft knife and cutting mat*
- *sticky tape*

What to do

1 Draw a cross shape on your card. The inner square is the size of the base of your basket.

2 Cut out the cross shape. Ask a grown up to help you use the safety craft knife.

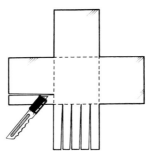

3 Score lightly round the lines that mark the base and fold the sides up. Unfold.

4 Cut out thin wedge-shaped slits on the sides as shown. On one side cut an extra wedge. The one shown has four wedges cut out. The box will need four on three sides and five on the other.

5 Tape your yarn in the starting position in one corner and weave round the strips, pulling tight round the corners so the sides are held upwards.

6 Change yarns as you weave if you wish. You can tuck the end of the yarn under the weaving just done and tape the new piece in where you start to weave it.

7 Fill the box with foodstuffs to give as a gift.

17 Hallowtide

October turns to November... the wind rattles the brown leaves before they fall dead on the cold earth; frost blackens the stalks of summer plants. The dark nights grow longer.

In the face of darkness, death and decay, it is easy to be fearful. Long ago, people were afraid that unseen forces of darkness and death were more powerful at this time of year. Some people find this a useful time to think about all the things that scare them, all the shadowy things no one can really explain.

But Christians bring good news: Jesus has conquered death. Anyone who follows him will be safe with God for ever. The evening of fear is called Hallowe'en—the eve of the day when people remember that a holy—'hallowed'—God has won.

The following day is a Christian festival called All Hallows Day. 'Hallow' is an old word for a holy person or 'Saint', so it is also called All Saints Day. It is a day for remembering Christians from long ago: they have died, but their life is safe with God.

The next day is called All Souls Day—a time for remembering everyone who has died. Whatever happened to people in this life, Christians believe that God will make everything right and good in the end.

A Hallowtide display
All around are things that are dead and dying. But the seeds that have tumbled from the seedpods are a reminder of new life one day.

The candle shining in the dark is a reminder of Jesus, who said, 'I am the light of the world.'

A seed must fall

One of the first Christians, Paul, was asked, 'What happens to Christians who die?'

'Think about this,' he said; 'a seed must fall to the ground so it can grow into a lovely new plant. So, too, a person must die so they can be given a wonderful new body. No one knows what that body is like, but it is just right for being with God for ever.'

18 Mary

Christians have great respect for someone called Mary—the young woman God chose to be the mother of Jesus.

The story goes that an angel came and told her this startling news. Her baby was not going to be the son of her future husband, Joseph. He was going to be God's son.

Mary was very surprised; but she was willing to do what God wanted—even though it turned her life upside down to be pregnant before she was married!

All Christians respect her because she is a shining example of someone who was willing to do as God wanted.

Some give her a very special place indeed: they have festivals to celebrate the day she was born (September 8), the day the angel came to visit with the news that she was to be the mother of Jesus (March 25), and the day she went to be with God (August 15).

May and October are set aside as well as special months in which to remember Mary.

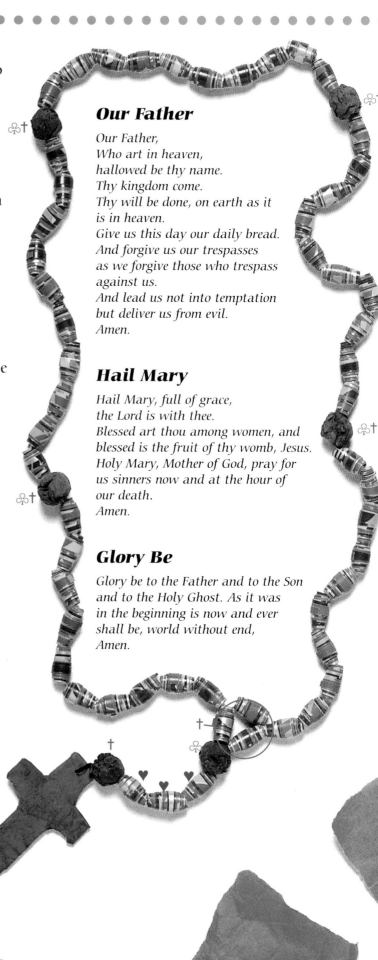

Our Father

Our Father,
Who art in heaven,
hallowed be thy name.
Thy kingdom come.
Thy will be done, on earth as it
is in heaven.
Give us this day our daily bread.
And forgive us our trespasses
as we forgive those who trespass
against us.
And lead us not into temptation
but deliver us from evil.
Amen.

Hail Mary

Hail Mary, full of grace,
the Lord is with thee.
Blessed art thou among women, and
blessed is the fruit of thy womb, Jesus.
Holy Mary, Mother of God, pray for
us sinners now and at the hour of
our death.
Amen.

Glory Be

Glory be to the Father and to the Son
and to the Holy Ghost. As it was
in the beginning is now and ever
shall be, world without end,
Amen.

A rosary

Some Christians have a string of beads called a rosary. At the beginning, the person saying the rosary holds the cross as they recite a statement of belief, the Apostles' Creed. The beads remind them of three special prayers they say:

- The Our Father is the prayer Jesus taught. It is said on the beads marked †.

- The Hail Mary is a prayer that begins with the greeting the angel first gave Mary. Each set of ten beads is called a decade, and the prayer is said on every bead in the five decades and the three marked ♥.

- The Glory Be gives glory to God the Father, Son and Holy Spirit. It is said on the bead marked ♣ and after each set of ten beads, before the next Our Father.

As people say the prayers, they also think about important events from the life of Jesus—such as his death and resurrection—and what these things mean to them.

Some Christians like to have a picture of Mary with her child, Jesus. This type of painting is called an icon, and lots of the things in it are symbols, with special meanings.

Above all, in pictures of the mother-and-child, Mary is inviting people to look mainly at Jesus. He is the one Christians follow, who makes people God's friends.

Make it!

You will need

- **two sorts of coloured paper**
- **thin card**
- **scissors**
- **glue stick**
- **PVA glue thinned with water 1:1**
- **a thin knitting needle**
- **needle and yarn**

What to do

1 Cut 56 long, thin triangles from one sort of paper. Take each in turn. Spread glue from the glue stick over the wrong side except for about a centimetre at the wide end.

2 Wind it round the knitting needle, starting with the wide end. Make sure the point is firmly stuck down.

3 Tear 6 small squares of the second type of paper. Scrunch and unscrunch them several times. Then dip them in the glue and water mix and scrunch them tight. Leave to dry.

4 Cut a small cross from plain card. Tear strips of paper, dip them in the glue and water mix, and wrap them around the cross to cover it. Leave to dry.

5 Use the needle and yarn to put the rosary together as shown.

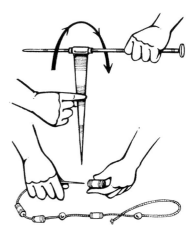

19 Saints

Christians believe that they are all part of God's family—both Christians alive today and Christians from long ago. Sometimes they call this 'the communion of saints'.

Shining lives

Here is a tissue-paper window rather like a church stained-glass window to remind people of what a saint is: someone who lets God's love shine through them into the world.

Make it!

You will need

- **2 pieces of black card**
- **tissue paper in several colours**
- **sticky-back plastic**
- **scissors**
- **craft knife, cutting mat and ruler**
- **glue stick**

What to do

1 Lay one piece of black card on the cutting mat and cut a window frame, using a ruler to help you get straight lines. Cut the other piece in the same way.

2 Cut two pieces of sticky-back plastic about 5 mm bigger all round than the window hole.

3 Unpeel the backing from one and lay it sticky side up. Carefully position one of the frames on top.

4 Now cut tissue paper people and arrange them one by one on the sticky side. Trim away any bits of tissue that stick out beyond the window itself.

5 Unpeel the backing from the second piece of plastic and lay this carefully on top. It helps to have two people do this, to hold the plastic flat as you lower it on to the tissue paper design. Glue the second frame on top of the filled frame.

Another meaning of the word 'saint' is a Christian whose life was a example for others to follow, and whose lives seemed to copy that of Jesus more than most.

A patron saint is one who has been linked to a particular 'good cause'.

For example, the countries in the British Isles all have a patron saint. On the 'saint's day' people may have a special celebration of all that makes their country special, and its heritage of song and story.

Saint George of England: April 23

No one knows if there ever was a 'real' Saint George. Perhaps he exists only in legends. Tales are told of a knight who killed a cruel dragon. Later, however, he was martyred—put to death because he would not give up his faith in Jesus.

Christians remember what Jesus said: any of his followers must be ready to die for what they believed in—as Jesus himself did.

Saint David of Wales: March 1

Saint David helped Christianity grow in Wales and went round from place to place teaching people and encouraging them. In the end he became a church leader—a bishop.

In the cathedral at St David's in Wales is a casket said to contain his bones. 'Relics' such as these are important to some Christians. They believe they are especially holy, and that God's power can work more easily in the place where they are than in other places.

Saint Patrick of Ireland: March 17

Saint Patrick helped spread the Christian faith in Ireland many hundreds of years ago. The shamrock is one symbol linked to Patrick: the story goes that people found it hard to understand how one God could be Father, Son and Holy Spirit. Patrick picked a shamrock leaf as a picture of 'three in one'.

Saint Patrick helps Christians remember Jesus' words to go out telling others the good news he brought— about how much God loves them.

Saint Andrew of Scotland: November 30

Saint Andrew is a saint from the Bible. He was a fisherman. One day he was at his work near his boat and Jesus came and asked him to join in the work of telling people about God.

Andrew went. Christians see him as a shining example of someone who was willing to take risks to do as Jesus wanted.

Saint Christopher: July 25

Saint Christopher is the patron saint of travellers. A story says that a child once asked Christopher to carry him across a swirling river. Christopher agreed—but the child was so heavy he nearly failed.

When the child was safe on the other side, he saw it was the boy Jesus. Christopher had been carrying not only Jesus but all the wrongdoing of the world that Jesus came to put right.

Some people pray to Saint Christopher, asking him to pray to God on their behalf for safety in their travels. Some people wear medallions showing Saint Christopher to remind them that God takes care of travellers.

20 Saint Francis

One of the best-known saints is Saint Francis. His life is an example to other Christians.

He was born the son of a wealthy family in Italy in 1182. As a young man, he had lots of fun enjoying all the things money can buy.

Then, in 1206, he suddenly began to see things differently. He was very rich; others were very poor. Francis believed God was telling him to change his ways.

Francis decided to spend all his life doing as Jesus taught. He gave away his money. He lived very simply. If people gave him gifts, he used all he could to help the poor and the sick.

Knowing God better brought him joy. So did helping others. He also took delight in the wonderful world God had made.

Animals and birds trusted him, and seemed to understand him when he spoke. Other people were moved by his example to take their Christian faith more seriously, and show more of the love of Jesus in their lives.

Francis died quite young, but he was not upset at the thought of dying. He believed God was going to keep him safe for ever.

Words of Francis

'Every creature in heaven and on earth and in the depths of the sea should give God praise and glory and honour and blessing; he has borne so much for us and has done and will do so much good to us; he is our power and our strength, and he alone is good, he alone most high, he alone all-powerful, wonderful and glorious; he alone is holy and worthy of all praise and blessing for endless ages and ages. Amen.'

Make it!

Make this papier mâché bowl to collect for the needy.

You will need

- *plastic bowl or tub*
- *cling film*
- *scrap paper*
- *wallpaper paste*
- *paints*

What to do

1 Cover the bowl with cling film.

2 Mix the wallpaper paste with water. The mix should be like thick cream.

3 Tear the paper into small pieces. Dip each into the paste, and then overlap them on the outside surface of the bowl. Leave to dry.

4 Make two more layers in the same way. When the bowl is dry, lift the plastic bowl out and peel the cling film away.

5 Paint the outside in a plain colour if you wish. Paint the inside to remind you and others of the need for which you are collecting money.

Helping the needy

Christians who celebrate St Francis' day (October 4) think of how they can give away some of their wealth and live more simply, so they can help the poor, the sick, and also any of God's creatures who are suffering. These bowls have been decorated to show concern for the natural world.

Francis and the birds

One day, Francis came to a place where there were a great many birds—doves and crows and jackdaws. Francis loved all living creatures, and he ran closer to the birds.

To his great surprise, they did not fly away. Delighted and amazed, Francis began to tell them about God.

'My brothers,' he said, 'you must always praise God, and love God. Just think how much God loves you—giving you warm feathers to clothe you and strong wings that carry you through the bright sky. You neither sow nor reap, yet God's good world gives you all you need to eat.'

The birds really seemed to be listening. So Francis asked God to bless them. He made the sign of the cross over them.

'You can fly away now,' he said. And so they did.

Index